Bad Kitty Diaries

Siena Norwich

Printed in the United States of America
First Edition, 2022

ISBN: 978-0-578-28835-2

All potentially identifying details therein that may allude to locations or individuals have been altered to protect the privacy of the author and other possibly perceived individuals. Any similarity to personages living or dead is coincidental and should not be inferred.

Bad Kitty Diaries

Siena Norwich

"If I love you, what business is it of yours?"
Goethe

Prologue

You're dead, Tag. Idle time made me a fiend and I looked you up. If you're like me you skip prologues. Innocuous foreplay. Take me to the heart of things.

Because you're dead in February, Tag. That sharp hinge of the world, closing darkness, ice wind. Pull your clothes against you. Your immovable frame in a bed. Sheets exchanged per passing lifetime. This was yours. Tag, you wrote about seeing your tenth grade teacher at heaven's gate in your book. Lines I did not absorb until tonight. Discovering your death nine months later, may I ask, was he there? At heaven's gate? That teacher you suspected was fucking the janitor? Was he kind to you?

II

You're dead, Tag. Pen discarded by me some years now, your death renewed a feverish pursuit of mortal anxiety, to create. Feverish may not be the most sensitive description, pending your undisclosed cause of death. The back of your book is your picture on a beach. Hawaiian hydrangea shirt, gray day cloudy like cold milky cataract. Wind tossing the bit of hair you still had. You have sunglasses on. Your picture evokes the sensation I am looking at death. No smile, eyes obliterated. You're on that beach forever now, Tag.

Cocktease. That's what you called me at nineteen. I don't blame you, the way your legs buckled as you walked beside me. "You know how easily manipulated men are," you said. None of this I hold against you now, Tag. In fact, you will be the only name I use in this whole book, after discovering your death months later. Some friend I am but I think you'd understand. I decided you would.

Tag, this book was halted for years. You would've wanted me to make it, even at the expense of my possible exposure. I am trusting my reader to keep me safe. It's easy to blame the dead man. This is the brave thing. We can laugh about it on your beach.

Caput Unum

I.

It began with my disease. A fatal incurable disease he did not know I had. First week in a new place. He was joking with men on the other side of a partition. He heard me laughing along. Elfish giggles, unseen and encouraging. Hammer came down. Found myself sinking into an eerie shock, thinking I misheard him. He made a joke about my disease. Occupying some alien confusion, my own laughter bit me. My greatest fears confirmed aloud that I was disgusting and unlovable. Repulsive and deserving of the lethal infection living in my body, my deepest cavity, my tainted viscera. A spoiled woman. All strings of affection dissolved, my mouth tugging a sob.

I hated him. Swore to all I was close I could never possess a single shred of amicable intrigue toward him again. My boyfriend was relieved. I was slightly. The power out of my hands. Yet the following days had the opposite effect. Instead of being safely repelled I was ensnared. Some great leaking insecurity made my voice crack when he came near. This is where it grew. It started with a cruel joke about my disease. He became my disease.

II.

X returned to my thoughts. He saw me crouching and I felt his eyes reach the curve of my ass. A day later he commented on my posture. Like a cut of veal, I was weighed in his hand. I found myself rehearsing the glances, reliving the words alone in front of a bathroom mirror, fearing someone may walk in and catch my lips rounding a whisper. Only I hear myself.

On his face. A real gem: a cut on his jaw from shaving. Picturing it. His deft hands press the blade in his jaw, and then the recoil, neck taut, eyes cast downward, inspecting the blood in the mirror. Its ageless color.

He popped a blade out of a knife the other day. I was toiling with it for twenty minutes afraid of slicing my thumbs. But he did it so easily, without thought. His certain calmness was crushing. Squirrelling myself away with essays on intergenerational love affairs, looking for something to articulate my impulse towards him.

We once bonded while discussing burning things as children. His eyes lit with joy as I recited how I mutilated dolls with sheer creative power and I understood his dien bien phu mud huts and matches.

There was one terror I knew in his presence on my first day. The lights went out in the room we sat. He stood up and I didn't recognize him. He became a stranger, something sudden and monstrous.

He prowls around like a wolf. Steps slow and heavy, head bent surveying surroundings. Says hello while grimacing. I chirp back. In our office he sat to my right. Looking in his eyes, I felt an almost indiscernible shutter. Some fear when I hold them too long. Sometimes if I stare too long his words taper off. There is something intense about him. Maybe it's the caffeine.

My infatuation is a pattern. It is a symptom of an unyielding sadness for secret things. Bound by fated incidents, roles, clustered with conclusions. Stuck in a formula. I adhere to the ritual, I am a slave to it. I know my weakness.

I consume less. I will use my body to transcend material limitations. Offer myself up to be assessed on the adequacy of this performance. My body will be too weak to bear affection, to see all love as a loan. This body of mine, this mysterious garment, longs to be completed by your mending gaze. The cruciform planes of my spine and ribcage will be an alter I prepare day by day.

Perhaps my lexical idiosyncrasies are a farce, my reader turned spectator conscripted into my protest. The contrary pressures of my longing and renunciation, of myself and this man, may realize a desire of spiritual repletion through self-annihilation. I will make these maladaptive behaviors venerated eccentricities, like daughters of fourth century roman aristocrats that became ascetics. No earthly suitor may do if not him, may will none evil.

Unfettered in the wild. Farce of kindness. I laugh along and encourage banter around me, the very pit of me repulsed. I crave forbidden courtship. I picture it carefully. Upstairs, especially quiet in summer. Like a church. Some lights burned out. Dizziness pulls at my ankles. But I wait. He loves to keep his feet quiet when he speaks out. To make me jump like a bad kitty.

III.

I'm learning something strange about myself. I'm harkening to an atavistic perversion. Erotic leanings, questing in psychiatric journals, perusing curious sites. Sadomasochism as my spiritual anguish, a great disruption of the prosaic order. Quiet and clutching myself in bathrooms, staring out from my desk like I'm not there. Sheltering religious objects of unattainable men. It's chilling to recall how early these visions set upon me. A worm in my heart, gnawing faithfully as I stood upstairs alone, begging him to find me. His steps tracing the paraphilic outline of my disease.

A thin shell of disdain keeps me warm. My nerves crawl into me when I speak to him. Breathy pauses, withdrawing into a fearless stare.

He told me not to trust him. The more I speak to him the more I believe there is some inconceivable pain he's endured that's hardened him. That passing years of disappointment, a great isolation he's worn like clothes, give him an invincible confidence. Sometimes I break it with my calm gaze, my silent watching. Like an abused animal. Holding myself in regal austerity like a statue, I grow cold waiting, plunging inward. There's a voice wincing in me when I'm alone. It curses him in the shadow of shelves. There's a vacuum pull in the stairwell. I dream of him finding me, I plead in isolation that I am stumbled upon. Discovered in naked solitude. And I dream of us facing each other, my eyes wide in fateful wonder. Eyes so wide I am swallowing him, inviting him without sacrificing my strength. I bite and bruise and bleed. I am not a statue anymore.

IV.

A mutual acquaintance went missing. We suspect some clinical pharmacopeia. X said he was glad this person was "receiving the help they needed and that by being there they must be better off than they were before". I told him this was a lie. Sometimes it is worse when you leave those places. You spend the rest of your life afraid you will return to the hospitals. Because you know what you're capable of. You know you can go that low.

Suicide. Drugs. Arrested. Year one. Year two. Year three. Wake at dawn for vitals. Shove you while you're sleeping. Door ajar all night for checks. Bed rubber tarp under bleached sheets. You cannot see your face in any plastic capped mirror. Too scratched up.

He asked to speak with me. Led me down a hall to an old room, in tatters, filled with crumbs of plaster and furniture knocked over. The entire time the shrieking of saws and hammering cranks consumed us. Two figures engulfed in chaos. He asked me to take a seat. Not to sit. I stood for a moment, defiant and daring until lowering myself. He conquered me. And I could imagine through that thin cotton shirt the hair that may gloss him.

I've increasingly come to find a thin bitter edge of distrust in me. He reminds me of a sadistic uncle. Knows the systems, its rules, its pieces and how they fit together. Covers himself in paper trails. He horrifies me, how ambivalent and calculating he is.

Thinking of him when I wasn't there. Tucked in bed looking at the ceiling. Dark thin dollar mart curtains pulled aside. One thread out of place and I feel an itch for him. Something strange and awful has come over me. A great breathing fire I've sought to extinguish. I am evidence. I can be older, with a degree and an apartment, and still play in the old confines. Linger in the same distinct parallels of attraction that haunted me since eleven.

Today he was unexpectedly warm. Bright eyes and I could tell, the way boys in high school used to look at me, like I was a talking poodle. His compassion is merely a building of pressure. I am a raging nerve that needs another raging nerve.

V.

And there I said it. I am documenting an affair. It will not, in all pinching probability, amount to anything. But I'm a master of affairs of the mind. Every scene a sandcastle. My cold wet

knees. Each article of clothing a sick psalm recited by my fumbling hands. I am humiliated and shaking as I do it. My knee rattles. I can hardly stand. I am looked at with surprise and pity. Then the lunatic kills me.

VII.

I feel a great sadness and at the same time, a great sense of invasion. Everything I do is being watched. These very words being monitored by some unseen individual in a dark room. Perhaps I want to merit myself more significance.

Maybe I've turned to stone. Limb by limb. First my skin tensed. Elbows ached. Fingers stiffened. Posture slumped. I grow bored with all people. I start to guess the outline of their thoughts, they deposit their fears in me, I become the receptacle of their humoral paradigms of tears and ejaculate.

If X asked me to dinner it may be weird outside this place. We wouldn't know how we correlated to each other anymore. We'd become strangers in the daylight. We wouldn't really hear a word the other said.

Capitulum Secundum

I.

I went to a book reading. An ex-junkie with a bad wig. Collared lavender shirt, unbuttoned to his sternum. Several pendants hanging across his chest, turquoise, a silver star on a thick black piece of twine. I grilled him, asked him about the complexities of characterization, gender power dynamics as an author, the temporal relevance of his piece, its capacity for social commentary, his own physical process of outlining. Barbarous classroom jargon. He evaded all my inquiries in a shrugging, circling pattern of speech. He was squinting, reaching aloud. His agent was there. A brunette in a floppy black hat, tender brown eyes that measured every sigh and stammer of the author. Swooning over him. Some noble nurse, some great nurturing embrace that will warm this rugged, splintered man. Her eyebrows peaked in concern while he recited his prose that she could mouth along with him.

We listened to prose and watched expressionist body performances about drugs and sex. I saw a woman in a beige thong leotard whirling about a stage, dipping to her knees and windmilling her arms, grabbing a pipe hungrily. His drug addiction was a romance. His writing masturbatory. And I was swept up lonely and stupid, longing to be recognized for my art. I handed my best and most complicated story to him. He said he couldn't wait to read it and I said "I don't care if you read it, just don't steal it".

II.

I am writing merely to alleviate the madness. But often this is not enough. Perhaps I am onanistic like the ex-junkie. Today I went to the bathroom and looked in the mirror and my eyes glittered with madness. If you'd asked me then and there of my own interpersonal state, it would've been an ugly foreign object. And that's what I've become. This organic mechanism, aching and breaking. And I urge myself to continue to wait for the moment when he arrives. And I look so longing down the hall it makes me sick. That I've chosen him as an object of my wonders, just like a preteen with my teachers. I befriended teachers, not classmates. That it doesn't matter how many classes I take, how many degrees I earn, how many jobs or lovers I rotate, I will always be bent on some industrious talent to destroy myself.

And he is the poetry. He is the hamartia. I dedicate all of this to him.

III.

My boyfriend and I ran into him. Book shop, door open. Chilly. Autumn. I didn't recognize him at first, his back turned. I gawked at the resemblance. And he turned. I don't remember if he spoke first or I did. I introduced my boyfriend. They leaned forward to shake hands. My boyfriend drifted to the other side of the room to look at shelves. Did not linger, did not small talk.

I stood there watching X, he laughed giddy, holding coffee in his left hand, he tumbled backwards slightly into the wall behind him. The men with him joked about the contents of his coffee. One of them asked me "Wait, you guys work together?" in surprise. He informed them we were colleagues. It felt like a lie. That somehow my age and stature was elevated. I made a cynical remark about my position. When I left he told my boyfriend it was nice to meet him. Outside on the sidewalk I let out an exasperated freakish laugh. Went to a rooftop bar eight blocks away and became thoroughly drunk in an hour. Impulsively bought expensive makeup, wobbling slightly as the counter girl brushed paste on my brow, self-conscious of my breath.

IV.

Last night I went to a concert with my boyfriend, a small but well ventilated venue. I was bored, counting every song. Most of the people there were median age of forty-seven. Nobody danced, some sang along. Most leaned side to side and stared with mouths shut. I was more interested in watching the people around me, watching the shifting hues of the light show.

Before the concert my boyfriend and I sat in the adjoining bar. We didn't know what to say to each other anymore and I could hardly hear him when he spoke. Sometimes even when I heard him I pretended not to so he'd repeat himself and we'd pass more time.

Yesterday my sister was talking to me about switching her medication. Like selecting new furniture. This one's too soft, this one's too hard, that makes me tired, this gives me nightmares, that makes me feel like I have bees in my head. I pretend not to hear the pills tilt forward in the bottle like marbles.

V.

I walked back into the room, four drinks in, and X was on my left. Nausea bloomed in my jaws. I asked for a white wine, just a little bit, chirpily requested. I took it and found myself lost among a dozen people, unfamiliar faces, parted off in chatting couplets, immersed in a hum of babble. Holiday party.

I went to the ladies room out of fear I would vomit. A great anxiety that he was all I wanted. And that is the true terror of all of this.

How deeply I long for him. I walked back into the room and spoke with a hennish secretary. She spoke of her daughter. I acted like everything she told me was the most interesting thing in the world. I smiled, beamed at her in complete captivity. Smiled and smiled. It was very important to me to show him that I was happy with others, that I was alive and warm and approachable. He stayed within his chuckling cohort of men. Faceless to me, all I saw were the backs of heads. My eyes flickered over to him. I felt we were both pretending the other was not there. And when the lights came on he walked out.

He said he had to take the suburbs out of me. I wanted that. I wanted him to pin me to the floor by my hair with his shoe. He has a magical ability of making you feel alone while other people are around. He sees right through me. Like some soft little weed to spit on. And I want him to spit on me, mock me, give me any attention at all. To see all love as a loan.

And I want to get out my scalpels, I want to peel back that face and see the real feelings behind it, not the crunching words.

My eyes watered with airy detachment. I've found myself encircling some low point in myself, where I become an onlooker at my own actions, a weak spectator. And he seems to have caught this in my eyes, turned it over for inquiry and remedy. How I've come to leech on him. What vagary impulse has grown in me? As though I've acquired new tastes into age, I've become intensely attracted to individuals I despise.

VI.

Drinks with a friend. I chose a bar across from his apartment. Four doubles neat. Banged on the door of his building, a man let me in. I went to his door. Banged on it. Nothing. Woke up the next day horrified. Spent days preparing for my termination. I returned. Nobody knew a thing.

VII.

Something atomic espied while we sat together. A dreadful slip of black at the top of my garter, my skirt rode up during a meeting. I derive great joy from torturing him. Yet he is resistant to me, sweet Catholic Boy Scout. Immune. The only part of his being he cannot seem to contain are his eyes. They tremble in their wide brown jelly gaze. But his mouth is firm and eager to ridicule. The man I long for. I'm sure he'll forget me. I make myself so cheaply visible. I hear his voice and it just might be my favorite thing. It makes me smile just to detect it through the wooden door. Its loping inflections, pitched reaches of inquiry, breathy observations. It's as if I am there. And while I sat by him earlier, I studied the hair patterns of his arms. I looked at the inside of his arm and thought how I would kiss that delta of veins. He's in a closed door meeting and the paranoiac in me fears I am being discussed, my edging wardrobe or my possibility of being transferred away from him, the prized daughter for three cows.

Capitulum Tertium

I.

Hardly made it to evening, clocked out and got on the subway. Felt so alive, a young explorer. Didn't know where I was going, didn't tell anybody anything. Saw a friend on the subway but acted like I didn't, he came over and sat down and I just laughed in his face. Oh where are you going? Oh I don't know, I'm tired of feeling like I always have to report to someone. He liked this, my eye kept straying to the clouded negative of our reflections in the black subway window. I marveled at myself, could he see the desperation in my eyes? Got off a stop before I intended so I could get away from him.

I looked into two neighboring bars. The first was crowded with people much older than me and I was intimidated, knowing I'd never get the bartender's attention. The noise would hide me and hurt my head. Then I looked in a cafe with hipsters with notepads and big round glasses crossing their arms at each other. I settled on a bar with a dartboard that ejected me a month before for an expired ID and a fight with the bartender. Sat at a table, did not fit in. Everyone there was much older, suits, briefcases, designer jeans. I had a backpack and a confused look of twenty-two. The waiter wanted to know if I was alright, when I ordered my drink he backed off. It became an experiment, sitting there alone, unsure of myself and drinking, chronicling every detail.

The women were cold. Women never seem to like me. Like they sense their own defector. Bought my drinks and headed out, looped the blocks. The rest fades in and out. I remember grappling with blocks of sidewalk, looking over my shoulder often, staying on the lit side of the street and being grateful the weather wasn't too cold. Bummed a cigarette in a storefront. Cried in a public bathroom stall. Two girls slipped a pamphlet on abusive relationships under the door.

II.

I've chosen him. Quite clearly, it's an awful answer to myself. But I do believe this has been mounting in me. Even before I met him and I only knew his name, I would ask others about him. One told me, "Imagine every type of bread you can think of, rye, pumpernickel, white, wheat. All mashed up into one. That's him." and something of that urged me with glee. A secret glee, a hidden one, like I was holding my foot down on it.

What does he know? Chomping chocolate bars in his dirty old chair. He's hiding something. All this time I've thought him some brute, moving about the shadows with brutal certainty, cold vanity. It must be so hard to be so tough all the time. Up there in his tower of papers. Waiting for my match.

III.

Is this where love begins? The uncertain silences? The prolonged gazes? I've initiated the fantasy into mind, registered it as a recurring image in myself. To remove all my clothes before him. Words getting increasingly mixed up with each drink, letters replace each other in concession. And does he contemplate, in his feral imagination, that perhaps he's come to inhabit a role of virile charm, a figure of dark portent. What a beauty he is. The way he lopes down the halls, his soundless steps, his intent brown eyes. And when we look at each other, our eyes become the still point of the ever turning world. All else moves around the eyes. But our eyes hold each other, as if in a dark disembodied embrace. I've had this feeling of him, the most profound looks in my life have been exchanged with him. I look in his eyes and penetrate a frightening depth. I can look in his eyes and know there is depth to plumb, a reservoir of feeling awaiting touch. And I want to touch that depth. Our first handshake was so intense and brief. A surging pressure of flesh meeting flesh.

IV.

Let me breathe into the daydream. We are together. And you do not initiate the first gesture, you are careful, perhaps afraid. And I take my clothes off.

"And what are you gonna do about it?" That's what you said to me, one evening you walked by me and stuck your tongue out. It felt sexual and mischievous. You spoke to camouflage your gesture.

I take off my clothes. I am bare, increasingly cold. My nipples harden in the air conditioning, pink knots. You come to me, and take me with more force than anticipated. Take my clothes off. Take me in. Make me your hostage. Put your lips to mine. How terrifying. Our handshake, the meeting of flesh, the patience of two worlds leaking into each other. You're more fair minded than I. You insist on perimeters. But maybe I've snuck in. Like a deranged burglar.

V.

My life up til now I tried to be the best worker, best student, good daughter, good sister. And it never meant anything. If anything, doing my best made the demands increasingly inhumane. I'm filled with a deep hatred for him. Because I feel used, toyed with. That I've let him into an amicable dimension of my nature and he has learned how to tickle it, make it swoon, make me forget that I'm nothing to him. Absolutely nothing. He is the first person in my life that I have met that so utterly has no attachment to anyone or anything. He inhabits a world isolated. I despise him. To feel so directionless, helpless, ignored, is a crime against myself. But part of his cruel ambivalence to me is what I admire. He has made me question myself, what I think I deserve, my egotism. In response I adopted an austere posture, that somehow to submit will bring me a godly calm, a greater understanding. An interior journey toward purification. I want to reach a point of personal achievement where he does not matter anymore.

A part of myself has begun to entertain visitors of morbid envy. I find myself occupied with dull tasks of noble diligence, pressing my fingers in folders, the glare of a copier drifting across my face. Ears idly attuned to chatter behind me, of some casual party to bid farewell to a coworker. Fruit tart preferences, a distaste for a particular jam, the adoration for a puckering crust. Favoring banal things, ridiculing the tangible. I've come to know something ugly and selfish in my nature, a serious bitter curiosity towards other women. I find myself inspecting their bodies with their backs turned, the tight curve of a young leg, the browned slender finger and sharp painted nail. Their shoulders shifting under their clothes. Their small dirty sneakers.

The one I've suspected wore cactus socks. I've come to despise her. Before Thanksgiving she professed an inability to decide where to travel, that she would take herself to the airport with her luggage and decide from there. Upon her return she mentioned Utah. She once announced a predilection for tequila. She's been to Indonesia. She's rather bug eyed, big brown like his. She has various moles planted down her slender neck. Finely waved hair down to tailbone. A Grecian freedom of movement. An artist. I despise her. I long to become her. To possess her figure, her freedom, her finances.

VI.

And I can already familiarize myself with my later fate, a hungry silence seeping into me. My hands cramming envelopes in drawers, slowing myself to pass the time easier. And I can tell, the sun will recede, the temperature will decline. I will leave this place with half the hope I entered it. He has cast me away. Like a boring toy. A defective pinwheel. An empty wrapper. Speculated and discarded. This poetry has no end.

VII.

I learned from coworkers at a lunch table, burnt pizza and soggy paper plates, that he had a lover once. A young girl that broke his heart years before.

What is this hideous fixation? I want to know everything that girl knew. His birthmarks, how his skin feels, the noise he makes when he orgasms. If he could give himself to girls why not me? I've proven myself the most precocious of students, marks extraordinary on a statistically national level, relatively appealing looks. But what? I've often wondered if he liked the younger ones due to their transient nature, they do not stay and he can enamor their innocence and they cannot linger, he does not watch the fruit dimple with rot, maturing suspicions. I wonder why he doesn't want me? When all I want is him. What did I do to turn him away? Was it my intractable nature? My heavy makeup, disenchanted by an aesthetic artifice that symbolizes a larger consumerist womanhood? That my lipstick makes me double-mouthed and untrustworthy? Smug harlot. Why not me?

They make him feel special in the scope of mundane adulthood, girls. I'm too questioning, too curious and intense. Too verbose. I lack the girlish simplicity he admires. And I shouldn't be ashamed of that. I've done nothing wrong. I've succeeded, devoted myself to my career. Garnered the appreciation of administration. Should I not look at him with my begging cup?

I cannot lose something I never had. But did I lose them, those cave-like brown eyes that reduce me to my most base elemental form.

Capitulum Quartum

I.

I have been doing some studying on exhibitionism and voyeurism as dual dimensions of the same disorder. I've found X to be a voyeur. He observes me. Derives discreet pleasure from sneaking up behind people without them knowing. There have been many times he practically tread on my heels without me realizing. He watched me from doorways. He watched me while I read. He has come upon me while I admired my reflection. He is a voyeur.

And I have been a serious voyeur myself, lingering downtown, watching him as he walks down the hall, documenting in detail his body as he sat beside me. Posture, foot movement, clothing choice, hair patterns. When he leaves the room I leaf through his notepad. Doodles of tanks and monsters. Quite juvenile. I have feathered myself into an exhibitionist, ornate makeup, particular sartorial presentation, nail paint, rings. He volunteered stories of sexual tension to me as I sat at my desk. He mentioned a divorced man in his office unbuttoning his shirt. He mentioned a man removing his pants mid-sentence. He consistently depicted himself as a beguiled spectator, an object acted upon. Perhaps the inert Catholic child in him cannot seize prey but merely covets.

II.

My friend says I'm trying to punish myself by attaching to a man who could ruin me. Perhaps she is right to a degree but I believe it is much more complex. Perhaps it's about the horrific primal pleasure, the vibrating tension when eyes meet. I wasn't enamored with him when I met him, more like idly intrigued. Curious but able to put him out of mind.

Then one day he called me a bad kitty. He said it twice, he said it smiling. It surprised me at first, we were discussing a minor mistake I'd made. And that's when everything changed. It felt like the first time in my life somebody looked at me, without knowing me, and saw me for what I was. A bad kitty. A week later I told a friend about it, a much older woman, and she was horrified. I remember, she lowered her fork from her mouth, broccoli nudging the tablecloth. "That's harassment," she said. I lowered my eyes to the bread basket because I could not tell her how much I loved it. Sometimes I wonder how many others he has called a bad kitty.

My boyfriend says I am bored, that I am seeking excitement in the reassuring banalities of a workplace. Perhaps they are all right and wrong simultaneously. That I'm outrunning a family that drains me financially.

Perhaps I am outrunning the ghost of my grandfather, whose sick immovable frame taught me to change bed sheets while he lay in them. From that quarter sized black hole over his tail bone, a bedsore smeared in Balmex. From counting morphine drops on his tongue. From how tight he closed his eyes and lost his English at the end. Howling like an animal.

It's hard for me to reason X. I am forging him in writing to neutralize some of the poison in my longing. I don't know if it inflames the wound or sutures it prettily.

III.

My boyfriend shoved me into the fridge. My back was turned and I remember the collar of my robe knocking a magnet to the floor. He threw money on top of my head and said I hate you. Then I remember vacuuming the same seven inches of carpet for twenty minutes.

I have lived with a man almost two decades my senior for several years. I once read an article that said intergenerational couples are 'queer relationships' because they divert main stream mating expectations; that a gay or interracial couple may not be as quickly distrusted as an age gap relationship. I neither confirm nor deny this perspective, I merely know my nature and the circumstance I am compelled to inhabit.

The next morning my roommate asked me if I was coming home that night, a question hinting at my lingering near where X lives at bars.

I said I would. I've been trying not to think about it. About all the men that have come into my life and used me, said low things to me, gripped me and commented on my body.

Memories invade. Of my grandfather that described in thorough detail how he lost his virginity to a prostitute when he was fourteen. Of my professor old enough to be my grandfather that tried to kiss me in a parking lot and then sent me an email calling me a cocktease and ball buster, telling me I had issues with men and that I know how easily manipulated they are. Of an ex-coworker that told me to go kill myself. Of a boy in high school who choked me on the floor of homeroom. Of an old friend twice my age that told me he hated condoms and then became sullen until I sat down on his bed.

That phone call after. You have a disease.

And then there's X this morning in a black windbreaker shining with rain. Walking brusquely past me, and his eye dipped to my stomach as I sat in my chair and I felt the most overwhelming insecurity, the most severe self-hatred and exposure.

My sister, who operates on a variety of prescription drugs for her moods, wanted to book a hotel room away from our parents. She asked me to pay for it and I did. She said she needed the time away, the time for reflection and isolation, lack of interruption and distraction. I did it for her. And I'm trying my best here, with what I have, not to unravel. She got thousands out of me.

IV.

I begin to walk as if inhabiting a dream, my voice low and disembodied, my gaze slow and blind. Aspiring to thinness, I want to be so thin that I disappear. Living dead, gaunt and graceful. Pale consumptive goddess. Fusing female degradation with martyr beauty. This terror steals over me, an extreme distrust and paranoia of others, that I am being taped, discussed. Truth is I don't matter to anybody. It was silly of me to expect myself to have more importance.

V.

My therapist called me a femme fatale, referred to my feelings for X as "obsessional" (not a word) and a "crush". He likewise volunteered his age to me with minimal solicitation after I informed him of X's age. Sometimes as I walk I feel my body tightening, stomach clenching, shoulder lagging, feet dragging. Perhaps this is life's great plan for me, to distill my hopes and then let them evaporate. A shambling expedition toward destruction, a pained cry for attention, preoccupies my misdeeds. Sometimes my creative center feels misaligned, my waning enthusiasm could denote a clinical platitude. Depraving my body of dense solids, smoking and drinking coffee to a preposterous frequency. The pathology normalized, "you look great, have you lost weight?" I want my body to exhibit the thinness symbolic of pure and elegant suffering. To make the outside match the inside.

Got a tattoo. My therapist called me sexy. I told him I do not trust him because he has no furniture in his lobby. That he is looking to leave any minute. My last appointment. Sent an email later confirming it. He responded like a dejected suitor, "I sensed this was coming…"

VI.

A girl I once loved re-entered my life. Not much changes in six years. She was drunk this morning and drunk last night. She described to me, "I will take a shower and within 20 minutes I'm drenched. I just barely survived a full day of work yesterday because I had absolutely no control over my hands and was pushing back a seizure for eight hours, trying through willpower not to faint. I had to do an easy and regular task of taking down a customer's order and my hands kept fumbling, like floundering fish gasping for air. The customer even offered to write the order for me."

That's what I got at 10:30am from her while working. An alcoholic clinging to the edge of life. I ordered her a pizza sent to her house forty miles away so she would feed herself. And then she disclosed to me she had three more beers and four mini bottles of wine. And then she told me I can't expect the love from others that I give.

I loved her more than the world once. Everyday together, she was my muse. Always photographing her, always writing and drawing with her. And then we had two threesomes with boys while drunk. She claimed that because I remembered it and she did not that I should have stopped her. That I permitted unconsenting trysts. And sometimes it haunts me. The monkeyish way she would bite the skin on her thumb. The scars on her legs. The slight gloss of hair on her arms. The way her finger traced the inside of my thigh at twelve.

VII.

The woman I loved is mad. She always was, but it's not my responsibility anymore. Fifth go around for her now, I can just see it. Sitting for hours behind that table with the dung colored wallpaper. Fill out the forms, agree to the worst parts of yourself. Signed herself over to their care. Her letters to me have become incomprehensible. She doesn't address me anymore, just flinging tedious substandard prose. Her promise in the past evaporated, the liquor, the many boyfriends she's had that I don't know of anymore. Our genital histories were once exchanged in feverish devotion. What I knew of her, she knew of me. It's been some years now. Once a gaunt tan beauty, I don't know what the years have collapsed in her face. If those eyes, animal wet brown, have flattened to the neutral drift of her drinking. She haunts me. The woman I loved and desired to become.

VIII.

I cannot seem to accept the dreary boredom of offices, this writhing in dust. The true fear I am confronting lies not in X's rejection of me, but in his lack of understanding. Every day I have to smother the compulsion to destroy all my artwork and myself.

Capitulum Quintum

I.

Affair A: The Artist.

He put his hands on my wrists while I laughed on my back. He hugged me close and I bit his shoulder. He made dinner. When I first arrived, I sat in his bedroom picking at the bookshelf. He changed his pants with my back turned. He is not the man I live with. He is not X. He cannot wrestle the flame inside me. He is too upbeat and congenial. Boyish and inconsistent. But he's caught between my fingers. I fear my professional unraveling in the tumult of his eventual attachment. He's a man and men are bitter creatures when life no longer suits them.

For now he is near. Sitting first row to my every word. He could be my lover. But I could not be his.

I borrowed a pair of pajama pants from him. It was raining but my jeans were not wet. All weekend I was smelling the pants. They smell like the dirty crumbling house with the narrow staircase and dripping bathroom. Mattress flat on floor, closet missing door. Fridge empty except boxed spinach and wine. That house could be fucked. Every surface. But I will never do that. He is too kind to me. It frightens me. He is not rather handsome or tall. Thin, tightly corded arms. Great sensitive hands, fleshy and veined, a ring and wood bead bracelet. Meaningless tattoos scattered on shoulders and stomach like a penciled middle-school desk. His background is laced comfort, multiple siblings. But no animals. His parents told them no pets, only animals you can rescue and nurture back to health. How does that change how he loves? He tries to expand my art set. Giving me pens with rubbed down nibs, all the same color. Thrown in my bag while I urinate. He once grew opium, one of his many projects, like woodworking and sculpture. I could be clay to his hands. To be unusual naked again, melancholy whore. Through and through, noblest philosopher since fourteen.

II.

I've grown away from X. There is still the electric surge of anxiety when he approaches. The hesitant gaze of both parties. But silence. No extensive conversation. I sit staring without book in hand. Lost the love for the page. Just gazing into space, imprinting the outside buildings with brief shuttering scenarios.

X recedes from my daily interests but remains a hazy goal. I wish to exhibit my art to him. But he cannot understand. He can respect and admire artistry but will not participate aloud. Scientifically, he will note minor details. He occupies himself with elaborate hulking machinery, lists of procedures to conduct interspersed with coffee runs and bowel movements. If you are what you do every day, his world is a cubicle with papers. Mine is but I look elsewhere. Out the window. Into the fantasy. I've been married a long time to my imagination. My own soul torments me, its unpredictable compulsions, the way its fever of enthusiasm seizes a pointless outcome.

III.

We climbed a tree. The artist and I. It was a spontaneous decision on my part but he was more agile. It took me more time in stockings and skirt. Once in the branches I placed small leaves behind his ears like a satyr. This felt like high school. Aimlessly walking about with a boy after school, exploiting any convenient path around to look at our feet while walking and talking about trite things. Kicking pine cones, smoking constantly.

Later before returning to our desks we went to a hidden alcove under the stairs. Dark, tucked in a recess. We stood side by side and he jokingly continued leaning into me. He smelled my hair but at first put his face in my neck. I stared forward like I didn't know what was happening, like standing still while a bear sniffs you. I liked it immensely. It struck me with the same shock and contentment other gestures he's made have.

IV.

X invades my thoughts, my fears and longings. Someone told me a girl was giddy with him and he was bizarrely buoyant in return. I can't be possessive. He is not mine. He is free to do as he wishes, see whomever he desires, live life with joy and grace. To fuck and fight and figure out how to allot his existence. After all, I live with another man. I permit myself myriad pleasures that could be deemed questionable to the traditional confines of monogamy. I withhold affection and information, jerk off to other men and sway between an overbearing sadness and frivolous mirth. I force myself out of the mire of my obsession through art, I create and achieve a multitude of pieces, germinate friendships with all. But why am I not fulfilled?

I have safely guarded any potential happiness with the longing of one ultimate untouchable fantasy. X. I am preventing my own future happiness. One cannot control one's feelings. And I grieve so terribly like a grim monk. My art and feelings are the horse hair vest, the tongues of a whip. And I beat myself every second I am alive to the point where the blood in my eyes prevents my seeing, my interacting. I become immovable stone, remote and hopeless. I want him and his joy. I hunger and grieve.

Love is the absolute testimony of our rejection of reality. I will show the pain and beauty that could be. I will live my greatest wish in my art. I will make it. I will persevere. I will not give in to these horrible aches of suicidal fatigue, the leak of despair, the terror of waking. I will not die. This diary is permission to relinquish myself. I will make music with my chains.

V.

On a Tuesday, the artist, the tree climber, messaged me. We met up and went back to his house. We drank rum then beer. He was eager for me to tell him what was bothering me but I would not. It was X. The drinking progressed, we stood in his art studio. Daubs of paint on the table, small sculptures and plaster shavings around. We stood in the middle of the carpet and he was behind me.

The floor was cold wood on my back. Some comment unfolded, something went awry and I became ashamed and gathered my clothes.

Rain pelted the window and he pleaded with me to stay. I did. We went upstairs and took a bath. We used my pink underwear to stop the drain. The water was too hot. He made soup to fix my drunk stomach. But I wouldn't eat it because I hate cinnamon. Then he knocked the bowl of soup into the bathtub and orange plumes spread around my naked body. I drained the tub, he undressed and got in. All hot water used up. Water gone cold. No sex.

I awoke with shame and amusement. His kindness increased my anxiety. I felt the urge to flee, to get out, as though I couldn't stand another minute looking in his face. But he didn't want me to go, and continued claiming I could stay as long as I wanted, even washing and drying my clothes to prolong my stay. I tossed and turned in a vicious hangover. He was better about it, not as slighted by the booze. Coffee. Bacon. The house smelled of it and there was smoke. I ate two slim burnt pieces.

I told him I didn't want to see him again. And I knew he loved me, he loved how terrible and messy I looked with my hair in every direction, the smears of last night's mascara along my cheeks, breath like mustard gas. I would close my eyes while resting and open them to see him watching me. This was a repeating occurrence that disturbed me. I left by two pm.

In the car the sunlight made me dizzy, the weather perfect. Visited an old friend, ate Greek food. He empathized, insisted this was an understandable act, "a blessing in disguise". I was too disoriented to disagree.

Home, I fell asleep. My roommate entered, resumed conversation about bullshit at work, minor fears and material annoyances. Then he told me he hoped I hadn't cheated on him.

The entire day I was preparing myself for a war zone, screaming and tears, threats. But he was shockingly calm about it, very civil and reasonable, claiming he expected something like this to happen, that we have a large age gap, that I am so young myself, and that I've been so unhappy for so long. He sat next to me, and in my half awake and exhausted state, I thought he told me "It's like it didn't even happen".

VI.

I ended the relationship with the artist. He looked at me as I sat at my desk as if he was looking at an old picture of himself. I am subjecting myself to penance, silence. That I feasted on the flesh and senses and must resume silence. Become hollow and stone. To cleanse myself.

I am mourning the fantasy of X, that my imagination more than himself is responsible for my love. And I am mourning the close friendship and bond I created with the artist in such a short time, and the pain I caused him. And there is some fear in there, although he seemed more enthusiastic than me to retain secrecy. He claims he is a pacifist. A fashionable socialist. I want to believe him but I seem to believe the volatility of a spurned man more.

I feel rather out of sorts and dispossessed. Cut off from everyone. From family, womb. From partner, pseudo-conjugal stability. From friend, shattered by erotic interaction. From my job, for having called out two days this week. My close friend said this is a transformative process for me. I am not seeing that. I am knee deep in blood.

VII.

I paddled myself on the bed. Swats of three then pause. Breathe between blows. My scarlet ass and thighs. I would lean myself over my bed at ninety degrees and hit myself. Or I would lie in bed on my side in an *S* shape and hit myself. Part of it was self-hatred disguised as a penance ritual. Part of it was erotic entertainment for myself. I discovered the kernel of my desire, what specific predilection unfettered my blood pressure.

My roommate in the other room kept calling me to dinner, groaning with every spanking sound. "It's weird when your girlfriend is just spanking herself in the bedroom".

Getting closer to numb.

The paddle was a gift from a man named Fox at a meet-up I went to years before. The establishment kicked him out shortly after because he was too violent.

VIII.

As I get older I contemplate the prospect that what I want does not exist. That my world is too small and I have not equipped myself to be calm with this pointless labor, circling tracks in sand. Part of me is angry at these false allegiances around me, sentiment disguised as politics. But I'm moreso angry at myself for consistently attempting to engage the sympathy and friendship of people who do not deserve it. People that betray me, belittle me, falsify my image. I feel misunderstood and used.

An ex therapist said, I am not taking care of my depression. A flashback to a seasonal appeal in my life for a clinical third party to validate my growing pains. I have been drinking more frequently, heavily every night the past weeks. Is there hope for me? Change comes from within, God helps those that help themselves what not. I say that's a lie. Some people do nothing to help anybody other than themselves, deceive and disregard others and walk the earth completely fine. Then there are others that earnestly devote themselves, try to puzzle and maintain a compassionate balance in their lives.

What happens to them? I am not content with protocols and procedures. False exceptionalism, fetishizing alternative interests, dull conversations.

IX.

I am not some office worker. I am not a payment made on time every time. I am not my funny colored shoes or my sharp collars. I am not my tight lipstick smile or my thickly bordered brows. I am not my starving. I am not my fifth glass of wine on a Monday night. I am not those three packs of cigarettes I bought. I am not my bank account I fear to check. I am not that ticket to the concert. I am not crying anymore. I am not the cluster of thorns. I am not that affair I had with a man I do not love or respect or admire. I am not that cramped bed of unwashed linen and dandruff. I am not my photo. I am not my degree and the guiding figures I have denied. I am not my strange conversations or my lonely weekends. I am not the swinger clubs with the weekend warriors. Those little windows for each room, you can choose to pull the curtains across if you don't want to be watched. I am not this place, with its stationary legions of computers and scanners, its dust copier, and its discarded snow globes. I am not my online chats or my vicious emails. I don't know this person. She must be eliminated.

X.

X looks through me like I'm not there. There's a cringing distance, complete ice. Silence. I will sit and conduct a menial task, ask him a question, look up and he is not there. Out like the wind. Silence. I've been asked to come in this weekend. Both days. No time for myself anymore. Come home tired. Wake up with never enough sleep. A dull ache in my jaw. A gnawing hunger. A sense of hopeless vexation. I don't think I've ever felt more disregarded in my life. I am not an insect to be swatted away, more like a hovering flea that an old dog lets rest on its ear now and again. To think someone as myself, with my thoughts, could be so relegated by individuals with zero conceivable talents, personages who consistently deposit themselves into a giant machine.

First a finger bone. Then an arm bone. Then it swallows the whole head. You're halfway consumed and you can't even kick your feet on the floor anymore to rebel. This place leeches into you, it creeps into your mind like a brain parasite to the point where you cannot comprehend a reality outside it. You are no longer in the box. You are the box. No trace of you left. Just a husk, pod person. Mundane and dazed, coffee in hand, shooting between rooms like a pinball. No real mission. No real faith. No ideals. Just working, you work to the point where you become ash.

You titter half mad with exhaustion, and then when the reprieve comes, the moment's breath, outside at home, your lungs pause. You cannot retain any feeling other than duty.

We are not soldiers. We are not sentries. We are workers. We belong to a bureaucracy composed of casual corpuscles. We joke about the weather, we admire each other's dogs and babies. But there's a ghost to those conversations. The friendly small talk is a fog, you start to know the fog of living intimately like your own body. You no longer need a body because the fog will insulate you, you don't need to touch, you don't need to be reminded. The sense of inadequacy is mocked as a signal of naiveté.

How dare you expect more? You are paid. You are lucky to have a job. You are lucky to have a home. You are lucky to be alive. Reinforce this rhetoric of fear in ourselves to pay the bills, to appease the invisible crushing fist that tatters every paycheck. One more line filled, one more idea crossed out.

And where does it all go? Did he dream once? What did he see, at the edge of the water?

Capitulum Sextum

I.

Tomorrow's an enormous soiree. Everyone of some administrative capacity is chattering with delight. They gawk at the practicing band, standing elbow to elbow in the vacant lobby. Buzz saw shrieking, men shouting. And I have not spoken to him today. I have become cold and rigid against my will, assuming a posture of remote disregard. Sometimes it's deliberate. I am good enough to exploit but not to promote. To praise at a convenient lull.

II.

Tomorrow's an enormous soiree. I am consoling myself with fantasy. All the seasoned aristocrats mingling, their glittering champagne glasses poised artfully in wrinkled hands. The suits. Oh god, the suits. Pressed fresh like bitter taffy.

There's the low hum of men's voices talking casually in large numbers in a small area. The light is pure and illuminating from the floor to ceiling windows. They are here to admire the interior, constructed for visual immensity and devoid of functional use.

And I am there unexpectedly. Uninvited. I levitate twenty feet above the floor, above their heads. They are talking and then the words leave them. Confusion, cacophony. Barefoot, like a condemned ascetic, I rise far above their tilted heads. My skin lit orange by a curtain of flames roaring from the oeuvre d'oeuvres table.

Outside people are trudging the sidewalk with hulking scoliosis inducing bags. They hardly notice. Trails of money behind them they must repair with a decade's interest. In the lobby, every article of modular furniture delicately arranged to accommodate preferred egress traffic. They sent a team hours beforehand, an ominous colony with gloves and cotton black trousers. They ensure the delicate predilections of the elite, maintain their neurotic isolation with every stamped napkin, pulling the scrim with their scripted names taut on the wall.

X will be present. He has a suit taken out and relished like a one night stand. Mixed metaphors determine a mixed mind for myself perhaps. She's all mixed up.

III.

Affair B: The Scientist.

Thirty-four years my senior. I liked the way he kissed my neck when we danced on his white living room carpet. Kids, divorced. Only pictures of the boy, not the girl in the large apartment. He still had possessions in boxes from when he'd moved in years before. Like he didn't think it was worth unpacking, that he didn't plan on staying long.

We took walks on my break. He would point out the shingles cracking on a new building and discuss his Spartan and disposable prandial preferences. He would eat out of a box in the freezer because then the only dish he had to clean was a fork. Always economic, measuring output and inconsequential detritus.

Once he told me, "You could have the keys to my kingdom" and I told him, "What if I only want a season pass?"

This greatly amused him as I sat curled in his arms in his lounge chair. Almost fatherly, stroking my hair. He discussed taking me to the beach as snow clung to the ground outside.

He was always calm. Men in the office held him to the highest degree of utmost reverence. When he would wave to me with them around him, they would all turn and confusedly wave at me as well.

He had the most contained and careful demeanor, always charming and tactful. It was when I saw him go giddy with feelings that I ended it. To see a man so composed and admired shift into adolescent glee frightened me. Like the affection of an austere man would be a debt I could never repay. No sex.

IV.

The second evening I saw him we got into a car accident.

He was taking me home, holding my hand on the armrest between us. He overestimated his space while merging into a lane on a snaking road. He could not see a small car beside us in his large truck. I saw it but assumed he already knew it was there. It was the first time I heard him swear. We pulled over and he got out. Exchanged information with the other driver.

When he returned to the car I kept apologizing. I felt it was my fault for distracting him, holding his hand and babbling. Just before I had called our relationship an affair. He did not like this due to its implied brevity. Then he asked me about my family. He called my father's profession outdated.

When I entered the apartment, my roommate demanded to know where I was. And I told him, now my second affair. He said to me, "You don't know anything about this man. Do you know why his wife divorced him? He could be a nutcase. He could ruin you at your job. You don't know this man."

And I thought about the car accident, the man so admired and coolly collected all the time, suddenly texting me to meet him when I got off work. That he just needed to see me. The man who never admitted to having a friend or confidante. Once in his apartment he told me I was the first person that ever entered it other than him in the several years he lived there. Boxes still unpacked. Once he told me he was fighting with his ex-wife and he threw a coffee mug out the window.

I promised myself I would never have an affair again unless it was with X.

My roommate went outside for a cigarette, I thought about the car accident on the way home and did something I never do. I consulted my bible in my book case.

I closed my eyes, flipped through the pages, and asked aloud "What should I do?" and absently placed my right index finger on a page.

Numbers 16:7, "You have gone too far!"

Capitulum Septimum

I.

Last night I attended a satanic ritual at a mausoleum-turned theater. I've been there before. Small place, hard chairs, no room. I was meeting a newly acquired friend. The first woman I've courted is my roommate's ex-girlfriend. A dominatrix.

The first time I met with her was three months ago, I bought her flowers and dinner at a crappy diner. I drank whiskey at the table while she was late parking the car. We got along well though I drank too much. Her birthday was next weekend, she invited me to go to this event with her.

First she said it would be the two of us that she would pick me up from work. Then she asked if I could meet her there when I get off work because she wanted to get tickets at the door. Then she invited a man she was seeing. A Hari Krishna tattoo artist and her termed "insane asshole".

I was fuming, hurt. I bought her too many birthday presents. Expensive face creams, exfoliates, oils, beauty kits, designer mascara, $40 gift card, bottle of wine, and a card I wrote three paragraphs in.

On my way out the door of work to meet her she sent me a message "Hey sweetie" and then asked if I could buy the tickets for the three of us.

My criticism of dominatrices is some may let their professions seep into their personal relationships. She once knew X fifteen years ago. She remembered him but I'm certain he doesn't remember her.

She asked me to buy her and her man tickets. I had to run to the ATM. On the subway I was reeling from all the movement. Got out and walked four blocks in a rough neighborhood.

I see her standing with this guy by the door. "I thought that was you," she said. I acted very cool and coy to hide my irritation. I smoked continuously.

II.

The guy was not tall and covered in tattoos. He had two stars on his temples. He said that's where his horns were. A rose on his neck, stars on his knuckles. The illustrated man. I have since learned he is dead.

He talked about a fight he got into in Oakland. He said he was on his way to a friend's house and had to pee, let loose in an empty street, a man came up shouting about private property and punched him in the back of the head. I asked him why he didn't just wait to pee at his friend's house. "Because I had to really fucking go" like I was a dumb kid, and they laughed. He said the man pulled a gun on him and that he wasn't scared. I asked him if it was the first time he had a gun pulled on him, he declined. I asked that if it had been the first time a gun was pulled on him would he have been scared. He evaded this question also.

He was fond of drugs, particularly psychedelics. He showed me a picture of his dog that looked as thin as him. Then the friend of mine, the woman, turned the conversation into making the guy guess how old I was.

I hated her for this, I felt like she was dwarfing me in front of him to eliminate any libidinal competition. She'd transformed my resistance to small talk into trivia. I guessed his age without hesitation. I've seen enough older men. He guessed I was twenty-nine and was surprised to find that I not only was not, but was a local. They never seem to think I'm from this place.

My friend talked about how she slept with a 58 year old man once, that this was a feat. We stood outside for an hour and a half because we didn't have tickets and the ushers were punishing us. Beside me stood a slim black girl. Short hair, long neck, calm profile. Nubian goddess. One eye blind. She gave money to the bum walking by. The bum asked us, "What are you all waiting for?" and she said "Life".

III.

We found seats in the back by the bathrooms, people kept nudging past us. The guy sat next to me and he smelled fantastic. The ritual began. Two people in robes wearing metallic painted animal masks with candles at their chests, leading a fat blonde girl in lingerie to a table at the stage. They tied her down, poured wine on her, and then lifted a plastic baby doll and stabbed it with a kitchen knife. Sound effects ensued from the speakers. I became increasingly bored. They crowned the blonde with antlers and led her by roped wrists. The screen flashed images of epileptic eyeballs and Edwardian cabarets. Bow ties, pinafores, smoke, white legs.

A gentleman wearing the largest mask with the largest horns, removed it and said that what we just saw was not Satanism but "Christian evangelical propaganda". He then displayed a series of slides about various incidents relating to the Satanic panic of the eighties.

He discussed the McMartin preschool, the proven lack of tunnels, that in fact there were no tunnels under the preschool to smuggle children to pedophilic sex rings, but just divots for burning garbage. He then spoke of a book called *Michelle Remembers* as a discredited therapeutic diatribe pertaining to the evocation of repressed memories. That the woman who wrote that book also married the therapist that co-wrote it. I found this touching.

My friend was trying to seduce the guy she was with. Something pinched my back. I touched it and when I withdrew my hand there was blood on my fingertips, my back felt cold with smeared blood. The muscles became sore. I left shortly after with a lie.

IV.

We sat on Constance and Joseph's bench, gnats sticking to the sunscreen on my arms. I followed the sound of bells to the park and found him there.

"Kiddo" that's what he called me at the end of our conversation. I decided to go into the city to have dinner with my roommate. His train was late, so I went to the park, sat down and smoked.

On my way out of the park I saw X, sitting on a bench reading. I pulled a cigarette from my bag and came over, said hello, he seemed happily shocked. I asked if it was okay if I sat down, if he minded the smoke, he said not at all. He was reading a monster movie magazine I like.

At one point he asked me if I was happy at my job. I assured him I was, he mentioned a performance review and he fears I'm not being challenged enough but he also fears I'm taking on a lot of work that isn't mine. Then he told some stories about catching people giving blowjobs at work. He mentioned catching people rolling blunts in the bathrooms. Liquor came up, I mentioned my preference for whiskey. The eternal boy scout.

An old man walked by, who knew X. This old man had apparently sat down beside X before and told him stories. The old man asked me if I was from around here and where I went to high school. He seemed confused I was sitting with X.

We sat on the bench and watched the darkening silhouette of the trees, the lights on the walkway turned on, specks of rain. He said to me, "It was good talking kiddo" and did this little bow, his head bent forwards and looking up at me.

V.

I won an award. X presented it. He cried at the end of it, choked on my name. The man I'd been thinking of for years describing me with my name in his mouth and tears in his throat. I was concerned after that he would despise me for cracking his masculine prowess. I feared he would hate me. But he was calm and kind. We have never spoken of it since. But at that moment, when that happened, I thought maybe he did care. Maybe he felt it too. I have a recording of the meeting. I listen to it when I am alone. It is my favorite song.

Capitulum Octavum

I.

We stayed three hours after work last Friday. I kept asking him if we would get in trouble and he said no. We talked and laughed and exchanged observations, criticisms, personal anecdotes, task oriented inquiries. Just the two of us. Entire building emptied out for closing. I was off the clock but still working. A common occurrence on both our behalves.

When it started he said, "The 'rents are gone" and turned up his music. He looked so damn happy. To be candid I was too. What was waiting for me if I had gone home? A despondent withdrawn roommate who is either always in another room or always looking at a laptop I bought him? A cat I rescued that prefers said roommate? A sexless dull existence where my only constant companion my sketchbook? I was glad to have a place to be, to keep myself busy and with someone I could laugh and talk with easily. Could one say then, that X was my Friday night date?

We are always shooting rubber bands at each other. It is a game. We aim them at each other throughout the day. I will run around the room and he will follow me. I will crouch and laugh and hide. He will hit me whether or not I am facing him. The romantic in me wants to believe these rubber bands are a symbolic substitute for cupid arrows. Or erectile embodiments.

I would come in early and we would walk together, still dark and freezing. Once he apologized to me for crowding my personal space. Once he pointed out the moon to me. The seraphim in my soul could not plead aloud my frankest desire for its continuation.

He will accidentally touch me. Or lean in close to me. Or ask me to sit in his chair.

II.

X started a strange conversation with me some weeks ago. He knows my age and insisted that, "Millennials are risk averse. They are the generation having the least sex and the fewest relationships." Other strange details peppered into the conversation he said included, "Most millennials meet the person they will marry at work" and "If there is someone at work you would like to spend time with, don't be afraid of that and let that hold you back". Furthermore, he has started talking about babies.

My roommate has been asking me to marry him for years and I reject every proposal with rabid determination. I have not referred to him to anyone as a boyfriend for two years. I call him roommate, the individual I cohabitate with. Not the man who makes me cry or shoves me into the fridge.

III.

Two months ago we were both outside. I asked him if he wanted to see my garden. A plot of land near our building I like to smoke, encircled by vegetation and almost completely hidden. There are concrete steps at an iron gate to enter.

He followed me to my garden, I felt like a child leading him. We got to the steps but did not descend. It was sad for a moment, but briefly we both looked out at the garden in silence side by side. The beautiful solitude. What could have been.

IV.

The one quality about him that irritates me enormously at this time, however, is that he always has to be the expert in the room. The other day I affirmed Chaucer was a medieval writer but he insisted Chaucer was Renaissance due to our delineated perimeters geographically of where art movements begin that neglect other parts of Europe. He can talk you in circles with semi-related facts, he will turn the conversation toward subjects he knows deeply in exchange for disagreement. He always has to be the expert in the room. But I will let him have this. Perhaps he is the greatest expert of all for having claimed my heart.

FINIS

www.ingramcontent.com/pod-product-compliance
Lightning Source LLC
Chambersburg PA
CBHW010644100726
47900CB00011B/2969

* 9 7 8 0 5 7 8 2 8 8 3 5 2 *